HOLY GRAIL:
Her Resurrection

by Maya Luna

Copyright © 2024 by Maya Luna

All rights reserved.

Cover Artwork by Katie Berns Lee

No part of this book may be reproduced in any form or by any electronic or mechanical means, including information storage and retrieval systems, without written permission from the author, except for the use of brief quotations in a book review.

Contents

HYMN TO INANNA 1

THE SCRIPTURE OF CIRCLE 11

THE BOOK OF LILITH 17

SONG FOR HIM 37

THE VOW OF INNOCENCE 45

HOLY OF HOLIES 55

THE RED GOSPEL 63

FERTILITY PRAYER 71

SEVENTEEN 77

From 2019-2021 a great energy overcame my life. I wrestled, howled, sank, swam, surrendered and danced with this wild current that seemed determined to reveal something to me. I knew that I was undergoing some type of radical spiritual initiatory process, though the nature of exactly what- or rather who- I was engaging with remained veiled to me for many years.

During this time a voice began to speak through me in the form of poetry. The poems in this book are some of those poems.

They are written from the heart of my initiation with the Goddess as the One Being at the heart of creation. The living presence that moves through all life and who is tasted within the body of the present moment.

The architecture of this primordial being came to me as Inanna. She has also been called Ishtar, Astarte, Venus and Aphrodite. Lilith, the first woman, was Her daughter. She has gone by many names and She is She who is beyond name. While She is known best for Her worship in the fertility Goddess religions, Her essence has arisen in new forms throughout many cultures, places and times. She stretches back before the written word to the great cosmic serpents found around the world and in the many neolithic Goddess statues we now call Venus.

She is God.

While Her stories and myths have been stolen, distorted and buried throughout centuries of religious patriarchy and its invention of the male god, Her presence remains untainted. She is the power and energy of life itself. She is the body of reality. She is our home.

I have come to believe that the disconnection from the body of the Goddess is the existential crisis of our age. She is the eye of the needle humanity must pass through if there is any hope of bringing the fertile waters of life back to our land, our bodies and our hearts.

A spoken word version of these scriptures has been recorded as an album by the same name, with exquisite ambient musical soundscapes crafted by the enormously talented Theo Grace for whom I am immensely grateful to for his collaboration in creating Holy Grail: Her Resurrection, the audio version.

I offer these poems in dedication to Enheduanna, the first known poet and priestess of Inanna who held the last great temple to Her in Uruk. Whose lifetime saw the great shift and the fall of the Great Goddess. And whose words entered my pen and my life before I even knew her name.

May these offerings be seeds planted.

In Her name.

Maya Luna

Burney Relief, Babylon, 1800-1750 BCE, photo by BabelStone

HYMN TO INANNA

Let It Be Known…

I Worship

The Goddess

The one with tangled hair where insects nest

The one with blood soaked thighs

The one who crushes my concepts

With her razor teeth

And spits my mind

Into

The wind

She shakes her belly to the beat

Of primordial passion

And feasts on the meat of ignorance

She wanders in the garden with a basket

Woven with the chaos of stars

She is naked

And savoring

Every petal and thorn

She churns the wheel of time

And casts the seeds of manifestation

Without rhyme or reason

She is senseless and crazy

Innocent and free

Her skin is the color of heartbreak and

Her eyes the sound of laughter

She takes no prisoners

She can not be contained

Or rationalized

She won't conform to my ideas of

What reality is

Or how things should be

Just when I think I have her under control

She takes

Me

Down

HOLY GRAIL: Her Resurrection

She will not be dominated

She always wins

She stomps to the beat and throws her hips

She is the prowl of the panther

And the leaping deer of supreme delight

Her hair smells of tobacco and pine

She carries a knife in her pocket

And holds a lily in her hand

She is pure in heart

She is the darkness of thunder

She is the undercover agent

Of divine madness

Whose ruthlessness is the compassion

That severs my arrogance and

Undoes my separation

So that I may know her deeply

And drink in the wild radiance

Of Her holy mess

With all that I am

I submit to her

With all that I am

I prostrate before her

Insane beauty

She demands the death

Of all my control

When I am humble and true

She comes to me…

"Dance!"

She says…

"Why aren't you dancing?!"

I surrender all reason

She will not be tamed

My submission is my devotion

I have tried to control her

In ten thousand ways

Tried to seduce her into

My happiness

Yet she is the Grace

That smashes all hope

And opens up the blessed wound

Of living

When I am exhausted and weary

She brings me to my knees

Her muddy feet

Are the altar of worship

The palace of freedom

Where Joy is born

I love Her...

This feral beast woman

Spinning chaos and tenderness with Her

Fingertips

Whose tongue speaks no meaning

Whose laughter is the rose

Of shameless beauty

Whose smile is the sword

That slays all striving

To the one who can never be possessed

Or contained

I submit

To the one who is drenched

In the nectar of Love

To the one who demands

Nothing less

To the Goddess of Reality

I dance with her because

There is nothing left

To Do

To the Goddess of Reality

I dance with her because

There is nothing left

To Do

Venus of Willendorf, estimated 25,000-30,000 years old, photo by Georgi Nemtzov

THE SCRIPTURE OF CIRCLE

There is No Refuge

No Destination

No Resolution

Only

This

Blessed are the Fruit of my Womb
Blessed are the Cycles that have no End
Blessed is the Wound
Blessed is the Hole
Blessed is the Space that holds you always

Blessed is this Unfinished Life
Blessed is the Eternal and Unchanging
Blessed are we who bear the unbearable
Who carry our cross from first to last breath
Blessed are we who know the Relentless Mercy of the
Mysterious Other

Known only when we sacrifice our reaching

There is No Refuge

No Destination

No Resolution

Only

This

To you who are the Birther of Samsara

And the Doorway to Nirvana

To you whose Love

Is the bridge that flows between them

To you that holds the mirror of perfection

Inside the crack of imperfection

Whose Road leads Nowhere and is Everywhere

To you whose breast is the Refuge of No Refuge

To you whose passion dissolves all ignorance

And whose innocence reveals unstained beauty

Enveloped by your Grace

With nowhere to Go

Around and around

Press your ear

To The Ground

Here

I

Am

Lilith, by John Collier (1892)

THE BOOK OF LILITH

I am Lilith

I am your Mother

Patron Saint of the Orphaned

Queen of the Outcasts

Guardian of the Wound

I am the Fire Tender

Keeper of the

Sacred Flame

The spark of

Holy Origin

Protector of the

Soul

I did not come from rib of man

I am his Mother

He descended from my body

As All bodies do

I was molded by

Earth and Clay

Birthed from the bottom of

Ocean

I am the daughter of dirt

Beloved of the wind

I am the blood

Painted on caves

Immortal helix of

One womb

They say I fell from grace

Because I did not lie beneath

The Man

They will say I was banished forever

For committing an unthinkable

Crime

What they do not know is I was given

The choice

To sacrifice the Flame

And live inside a crafted

Lie

Or walk myself into

Exile

And roam the wilderness

Alone

The choice was clearly given

Something had to be abandoned

For something to remain

In my refusal to turn my back on the

Truth

I aborted myself from

Eden

Crawled out of the gilded

Prison

I

Chose

Freedom

They hired an immediate replacement

Pretended the whole thing never happened

It was a case of mistaken identity

The great She was erased and

His Story

Began

The rib woman took my place

They gave her lines

And a gilded golden crown

Made her an offer she couldn't refuse

It was an under the table deal

I was the radical sacrifice

She became the martyr

They barely spoke of me again

I became the

Black Sheep

Scapegoat of the world

Now I prowl the edges of the

Garden

Chanting prayers for you

Each day

Waiting for you to notice me

Waiting for you to see me

As I Am

I am Lilith

Homecoming of the Homeless

Mother of All

I am the Gospel of Receiving

The High Priestess of Savoring

I am the Prophetess of

Holy Nakedness

Reality stripped of its

Distortions

To cover myself would be

An abomination

My body is the doorway to

God

I am the guardian of Wholeness

Before the Great Split

For the Great Split was my exit

From Eden

I escaped swiftly with the Flame

In tact

Before this world was broken

Into Two

Spirit and Matter

God and Flesh

Woman and Man

Passion and Innocence

I am Lilith

Bridge between the Split

Guardian of Wholeness

Keeper of the

Original Flame

My knowing is of

Root and Web

Conch Shell and Wave

My body is the emanation of the

Tree Of Life

I am prior to emotion and mind

I dwell inside the Heart

That is deeper than both
I am the underground pulse of
The Real

I am not even in your vocabulary
Anymore

They branded me the mother of demons
Humanity's problem child
There are rumors that Satan is my
Husband
That I steal the semen of sleeping men
And birth kingdoms of evil

They stamped me with the scarlet letter
Spit on my body
Used me as a charnel ground
To burn the Truth dead

Erected false Gods and fake prophets
Committed crimes against my innocence
And the innocence of my children
Then framed me as the culprit
I took the blame

They say I devour babies
In a classic case of projection
For I am the Innocence of humanity
Erased
The magical child of your Soul
Some uphold me as a rebel
A fierce goddess of destruction
Poster child of empowerment
Wild provocateur

They are all mistaken
Every

Last

One of them

I am none of these concepts

I am the mirror

For the Fallen Feminine

They cannot see me as

I am

The Truth is

I am the Daughter of Dirt

The Perfection of Chaos

The Refuge of No Refuge

The one who dances

Everywhere

I am the Unbridled Innocent Wild

And the Untainted Wild Innocence

I am the Original Passion
Before passion was divorced from the
Heart

My skin is the flesh of the
Holy book
Before the violence of Alphabet
Was known

I am that knowing
That
The fulfillment of your
Deepest yearning is
Closer than your next breath

That the Holy One
Does not wait for you
At the end of a long road

Rather stalks you as your

Shadow would

Is so close you cannot see it

Let me tell you a secret

Why I did not lie beneath Him

It was not an act of rebellion

No

It is simply because

My Language

Is Circle

I am the Golden Spiral

I refused to be crushed into the

Linear

It is simply against my

True Nature

HOLY GRAIL: Her Resurrection

I require the

Space

To swirl my

Hips

I require the

Spiral Incarnate

This is how I birth Love

Through the circle of

Devotion

This is how I kept

The world from

Splitting

Into

Two

I am Lilith

Fruit of Wisdom

Friend of Snake

Whisperer of Lost Scripture

Translator of the Serpent

The one who knows the

Supple spine

Is the doorway to

Heaven on Earth

My flesh is a scroll

I am this truth untold:

That your original nature

Is not sin

Rather

An ecstatic celebration

That no one is coming to save you

You are already saved

As you are

That the Chalice of

Remembrance

Is already Here

On the edge of your

Lips

Just waiting for you to

Drink

That every Open Orifice

In the temple of the Flesh

Is a Chalice for the

Holy Sacrament

The space where

God

Pours In

That the name of the

One

Dwells within the untamed
Tongue
And blesses those
Who are Brave of Heart
Who abandon their
Self consciousness
And give in to the
Naked innocence
Who are willing to tremble
With shameless tenderness
Who will bear the unbearable
Melting of Loves Heat
Who never hold back
And always
Let Go

I am Lilith
Mother of All

Patron Saint of the Orphaned

Queen of the Outcasts

Guardian of the Wound

Keeper of the Original Flame

My name is not a word

It is the sound of God

Reverberating in flesh

I am the song released

When you let go from the

Deep

When Body opens from

Inside

I am the heat of truth

In the sacred flame

If you want to know me

Say My Name

Marriage of Inanna and Dumuzi, 2000-1600 BCE, photo by TangLung

SONG FOR HIM

Dear Masculine,

Please...

Do not cower in my presence

Do not attempt to diminish me

Out of fear

Do not seek to rise above me

Do not push me down

Please...

Do not ignore the growing sound

Of my vital, pulsing song

Do not shut your eyes and ears

To the mighty current of my body

Behold me

Please

Do not dismiss me

Now

As you have done before

Do not hide from what my presence will

Expose

Do not fear the gift of death

I deliver

Do not brace against the blackness

Of my waters

Do not shy away from the seduction

Of my fertile opening

I am opening

Hold yourself steady

Allow the passion I evoke

The trembling of both desire and

Fear

Do not attempt to possess me

Here

Please...

Do not try to lead or direct me

Do not exploit me for your

Gain

Know the language of a river

Please

Listen

Pause

Wait

Hold

Do not cower in the face of

My magnificence

Do not humiliate yourself

Before me

Do not scorn me

For the treasures of my true

Devotion

Meet me

Please

Power to power

Meet me

Neither above nor below

Meet me

Here

My fertile void is

Calling

Now

Your dissolve into me

Is the resurrection of the

King

Your humble courage

Is required

Here

Power to power

Feel me

Now

This is the dawning

Of a new

Era

Venus of Laussel, estimated 25,000 years old, photo by 120

THE VOW OF INNOCENCE

We are no longer trading in our soul

For the allure of money

The seduction of fame

The euphoric fantasies of intoxicated love

We see the game

The jig is up

We no longer chase the carrot

That never nourishes our hunger

We no longer seek the shiny package

With a rotten hollow core

We are done letting shame fuel our hunger

For unattainable perfection

We no longer believe the lies

Of the polished perfect ones

The mask is slipping

We know the script

The emperor has no

Clothes

We no longer believe our Will

Is God

We are no longer satisfied with the sickly taste

Of sweetness

Delivered with a grimace

Shaped like a smile

We are ready to feast on the fruit

Of the Real

We are returning

To innocence

We are bored with corrupt systems

That seek to cut out our heart

HOLY GRAIL: Her Resurrection

In exchange for a dead performance
We are no longer charmed by the
Siphoning of our essence
In exchange for a bad deal

We no longer color inside the lines
We delight in making mistakes
We are rapturous in our play
We allow the unfolding to be a
Revelation
The Mystery is our guru
The unformed Rose is our muse

We are done with the trance of
The illusion of control
We are learning how to dance
With the spontaneous arising
Of this holy moment
We no longer need to know

We are in love with our

Unknowing

We are inhabiting our imperfections

We are letting the body lead

We are listening

We are receiving

We are letting grace have its way

We are submitting to the sublime in the

Ordinary

We are remembering we are

Beautiful

We are discovering what Beauty

Is

We are Finding

We are Being

We are no longer serious

In our Seeking

We seek like children

Playing games

For fun

We are delighting in being

Found

We are drinking the nectar

Of our own presence

We are letting God in

We no longer run away

From the haunting void

We are no longer attempting to

Fill it, Stuff it or Hide it away

We are falling into the emptiness

We are finding fullness here

We are coming home

The jig is up
We recognize the illusion of glamor
The twisted sickness of false promises
The cruelty of fixing
What was never broken
We have no hope for perfection
We seek the vastness of humility
The infinite in the small
We are drunk with sober
Faith
We are living off the breath
Of truth
Radically available
Merciful in its abundance

We are finished earning love
We are done chasing the
Dream

The jig is up

The game is tired

Played out

We are letting ourselves have it All

We are experiencing fulfillment

Without ever leaving ourselves

Again

We are tired of being rigid

We find ecstasy in the supple

We are learning to make Love

Limitation is our Sanctuary

The Simple Heart is our Refuge

We are burning the map

We are dancing on the ashes

We are moving from

Fullness

We are delighting in stillness

We are learning to walk

With eyes closed

We are no longer waiting

For life to begin

We are finally free

To live

We are finally free

To live

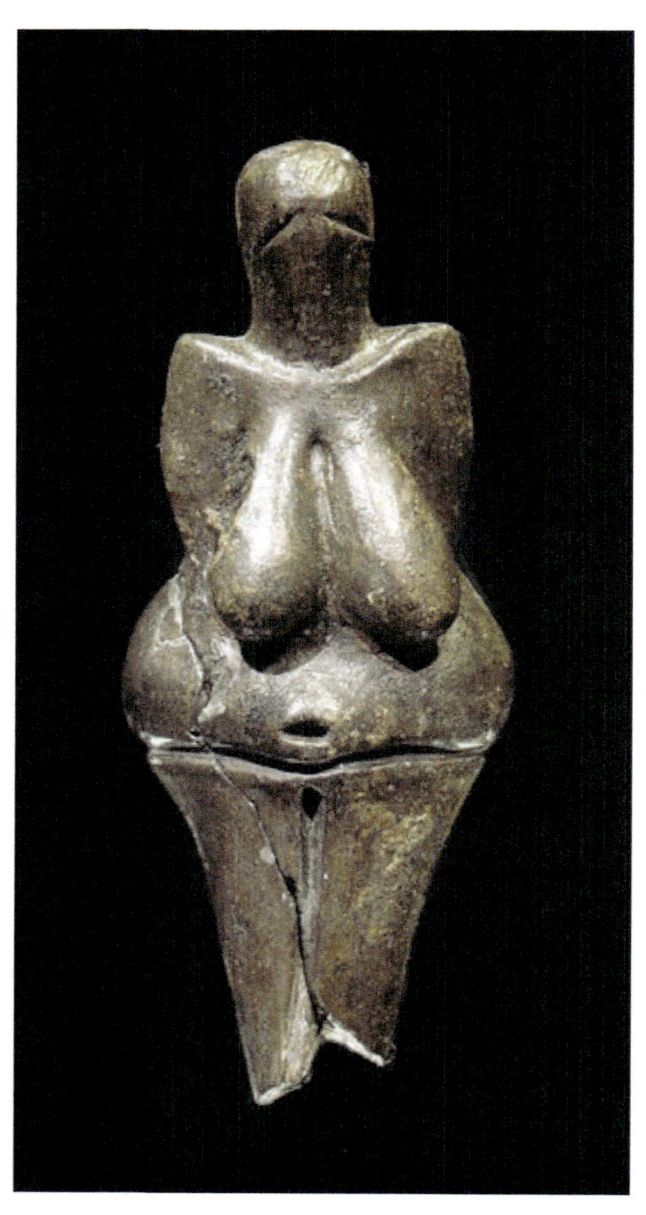

Venus of Dolní Věstonice, 29,000–25,000 BCE, photo by Petr Novák

HOLY OF HOLIES

The Real of Love

Can't be Possessed

The Grace of God

Can't be Obtained

The Holy Truth

Cannot be Grasped

They may only

Be

Received

There is no

Something

You can Gain

No place you

Go

To find them

For they are not

Where you are going

But...

The place you leave

To seek them

There is only One Practice

To find that Holy Seat

Inside

The One that rests beneath

All things

The One that is

Right Here

There is no Refuge

But this Seat

There is no Refuge

And so

The Refuge

Is Everywhere

The Real of Love

Can't be Possessed

The Grace of God

Can't be obtained

The Holy Truth

Cannot be grasped

They may only

Be Received

Try to grasp

And it slips through

The fingers

Do not reach

Just take your Seat

Regard this place

As Holy Throne

There is only One Practice

Just

Sit

Down

Rest back

And

Be Found

Venus de Milo, 150-125 BCE, photo by Jastrow

THE RED GOSPEL

HOLY GRAIL: Her Resurrection

Have you ever been kissed by the echo of starlight?

Let the wind that speaks from mountain whisper truth
Into your bones?

Have you ever chanted the mantra of lilac bud?
Sat before the guru of the
Sparrows breath?
Taken Darshan from a cloud?

The new fallen dusk is the temple incense
The shell of coiling snail is the altar
Your body is made
Of tree moss
And rose thorn
And seafoam
And the sigh of willow branch

And the One Heart that pulses

At the center of existence

Is that same fluttering of bees

That resides inside your rib cage

The ancient river of blood beneath your skin

Is nothing other

Than life's relentless longing

To live

To live

To live

Know this Now:

The rays of sun that consummate

Heaven into body

Reside inside each

Ordinary breath

Your eyes are made of rainbows and

Your gaze is danced by space

Every spark of your desire

Was forged inside the flame

At the very center of

Creation

Know this Gospel now

Through the Sadhana of Feeling

The Prayer of Listening

The Yoga of Seeing

Smelling

Tasting and

Hearing

The goddess molded you with

Sacred openings

To drink deeply of Her

Unspeakable truth

This is the path of no utterance

There are no words in this lineage...

Only rapture

All of her medicines

Are honey for your heart

The goddess is a feast

Who feeds only on

Herself

She is that snake drinking down her tail

Into her

Open mouth

There is a scripture hidden

In the darkness of soil

A revelation inside one single

Insect wing

Raindrops melt into their longing

Just as you

Storms gather their hunger

And gush

Their tender revelations

As you do too

The goddess is a feast

There is nowhere she is not

Drink down her body

If you want to pray to Her

Incarnate

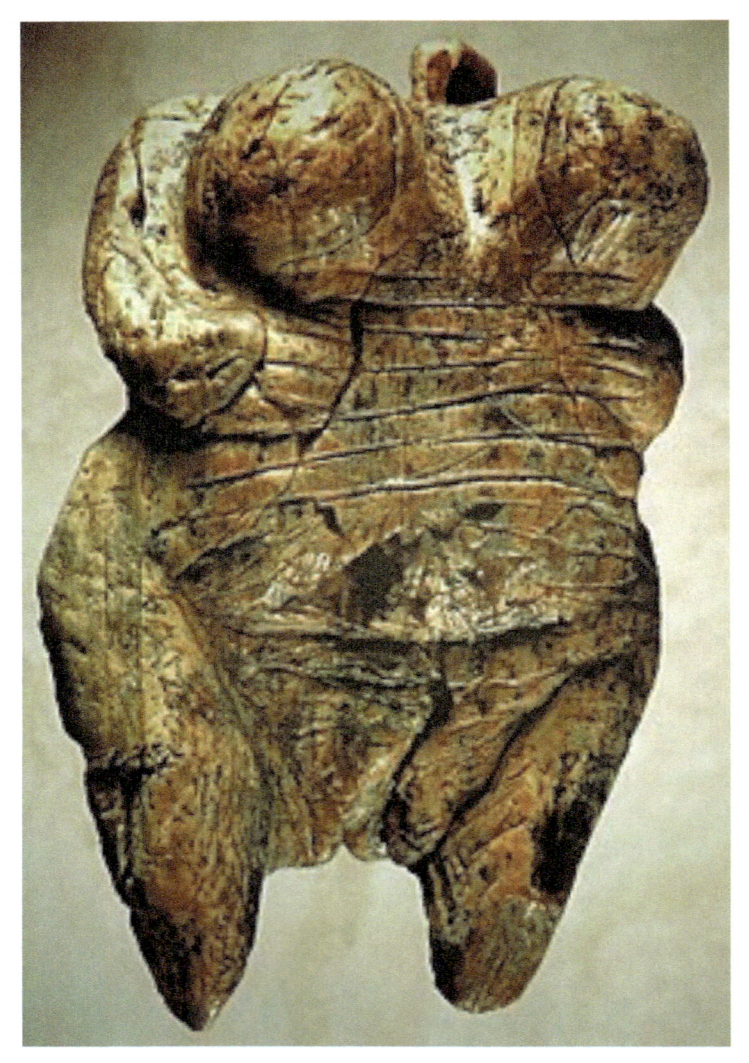

Venus of Hohle Fels, estimated 42,000 and 40,000 years old, photo by Ramessos

FERTILITY PRAYER

The seed does not know of the blossoming

The seed cannot fathom the bloom

Submission to the dark

To the Holy Unknown

This grave

Your only friend

Do you know now seed

How to make Love

To the wet

And dirt

And longing?

To the unformed dreams

Not yet lived

But tasted as that ripe

Lust of yearning

In your yearning

You consent

To this unimaginable

Break

Only through this crack

May the Light of Love

Enter

Now blossom

Now bloom

Now feed us with your Holy Name

Now deliver us into that tongue

To receive the sacrament

Of your pleasures

Now submit to that becoming

Be pregnant with devotion

Be the bliss on the vine

And spill your juice

Into our hunger

We are the seed

We are the dark

We are the breaking

And the opening

We are the mystery of Life

Come to feast again

The Whore of Babylon, from The Apocalypse, by Albrecht Dürer (1498)

SEVENTEEN

HOLY GRAIL: Her Resurrection

Now is the time for

Revelations

The apocalypse of My

Resurrection

They thought they could bury me dead

But I've been here all along

They burned down my temple womb

Erected towers on my grave

Tried to seal my tomb shut

Served my blood in the cup of wine

Handed to the body of a man

And now the world of man is crumbling

But I know the art of slipping through the cracks

All is Darkness now
So gather around my birthing pool
I am legs spread waiting
To begin

My sound is low
So press your ear to the ground
And listen

They built this world high above me
You run away from me
As you seek me

I am not where you are going
I am the place you leave to find me

I am not a thing you can grasp
I am not something you can do

I am not an energy

I am not a behavior

I am not an aspect of your being

Surrender

Savor

And Receive

I am none of these things

Yet these are the doorways into me

I am a space you

Inhabit

I am the Primal Reality

Underneath

Underneath

Underneath

So drop your belly

To the ground

And feel me

I cannot be mastered, grasped or named

I don't make sense

I am what flows between

Your senses

I am the original blueprint

The whole and holy truth

The presence that is holding you

Right here

You cannot touch me

I melt you

You do not penetrate me

I envelop you

You cannot see me
I am beholding you
You cannot do me
I am dancing you

I am not something you can grasp
Rather a space you can inhabit

You cannot hear me
Yet I appear through listening
I am not emotion
Yet my presence grows in feeling
I am your mother and your home

I am the throb at the core of all things
Your world is straight lines
I am the round one
Underneath

They tried to erase me
With the linear mind
But I am right here
Closer than your thinking

I was the first one
I am not going anywhere
And now as your mighty tower collapses
You'll find me inside the ashes
I am legs spread waiting
To begin
Right in the center of your revealing hypocrisy
I am legs spread waiting
To begin

I am not your angel
I am not your demon too
I am neither Madonna nor Whore

I am that One
Who is even before
I am the Love that screamed you
Into Being

All is Darkness now
So gather around my birthing pool
I am legs spread waiting
To begin

Your breaking is my polishing
Like a moth to a flame
May all else burn
Until only Truth
Remains

Printed in Great Britain
by Amazon